The Matterhorn

-

The Tragic First Ascent

The author: Ferdinand Kämpfer studies the bachelor's degree program in History, Politics and Society at the University of Potsdam. Since 2016, he has been giving guided tours of the city and giving lectures on the history of Thuringia in Gera. Privately, the author has often been to the Alps, so it is always fascinating for him how the rope team around Whymper climbed the Matterhorn with the simplest means.

Ferdinand Kämpfer

The Matterhorn – The Tragic First Ascent

Bibliographische Information der Deutschen Nationalbibliothek:

Die Deutschen Nationalbibliothek verzeichnet diese Publikation in der Deutschen Nationalbibliographie, detaillierte bibliographische Daten sind im Internet über dnb.dnb.de abrufbar.

TWENTY-SIX – der Self-Publishing-Verlag

Eine Kooperation zwischen der Verlagsgruppe Random House und BoD – Books on Demand

© 2019 Ferdinand Kämpfer

Herstellung und Verlag

Books on Demand – Norderstedt

ISBN: 978-3-740-763190

The booklet is dedicated to Benedict Perren, the descendant of the Taugwalder and Pen Hadow, the descendant of the late Douglas Hadow.

Table

Introduction 7
The story...8
References 57
Memory 59
Acknowledgement 60

Introduction

On 14th July 1865, two competing rope teams made their way to the summit of the Matterhorn. The mountain was considered invincible until Italians and Britons had the iron will to climb the colossus in the middle of the 19th century. The team around the British alpinist Edward Whymper won the race. It was sensational that for the first time people boarded the Matterhorn for good. But his rough aura was to take revenge: when the men descended the mountain, four of the seven climbers fell into the abyss, which is why the first ascent heralded the end of the Golden Age of Alpinism. What exactly happened in the crash? Was the rope cut? Were there any thoughts of murder?

With the booklet, the memory of the seven courageous ones is to be kept upright and the events will be reproduced. It is a kind of commemorative inscription on the 155th anniversary of the first ascent, which is intended to invite you to remember.

Ferdinand Kämpfer

The story

It all started with Edward Whymper, a young British journalist and illustrator who was sent to the mountains by the English publisher Thomas Longman to make detailed drawings of the Alps and nature. Whymper was 25 years old in 1865, the year of the first ascent of the Matterhorn, ambitious, curious and risk-taking. So it was not only when drawing the mountains from a perspective. Whymper made so-called first ascents to capture a full view of paper from the summit. So it appealed to the researched draughtsman to get from mountain to mountain as quickly as possible.

From the middle of the 19th century, the Alps found great popularity among the British. The so-called golden age of alpinism was born. However, since the 18th century there have been so-called first ascents, thus laying the foundation stone of alpinism. Swiss, French and Italians were the first people who climbed in the Alps.

The young Edward Whymper. He plays a decisive role in the first ascent of the Matterhorn.

Proof of picture:

https://www.spri.cam.ac.uk/museum/exhibitions/whymper/n5_Pic0001.jpg

As early as the 18th century, the Dufour peak, the highest peak in Switzerland at 4634metres, was named after the Swiss General Henri Dufour.

Whymper was considered an arrogant and bare-faced man who climbed many mountains but was reluctant to share his successes with other climbers. Among his ascents are the Barre des Ecrins and the Aiguille d'Argentiére, which the young Englishman climbed for the first time in 1864 with the then highly respected mountain guide Michel Croz from Chamonix.

But the king of the Western Alps remained the Matterhorn. It already impersonated the people at that time, was considered rough and uncertain, which is why many climbers did not venture to the mountain. Even Whymper had failed several times. He tried, among other things, to climb the mountain from the Italian south side, the Liongrat, with the Italian mountain guide Jean-Antoin Carrel. This quickly became clear to the Briton, so he informed the other climbers that an ascent in this way was impossible.

In the middle of the 19th century, the alpinists believed that the south side of the Matterhorn was easier to climb than the north site. As early as 1862, it was climbed by Italian and British climbers such as Carrel and Tyndal, after which the then reached peak on the south side was named.

Proof of picture:

https://www.active-mountains.at/produkt/matterhorn-ueberschreitung/

The Italian Jean Antoine Carrel, like Whymper, was also a somewhat rude contemporary, but he had great experience as a mountain guide, which is why he was highly sought after.

Proof of picture:

https://archive.benjaminschudel.com/nzz/matterhorn/index.de.html?mode=static

With Carrel, Whymper decided to make another ascent over a different route. But before it happened, Carrel jumped off. The reason for this was the Italian engineer Felice Giordano, whose services Carrel had been in for a long time. In addition, the weather in the summer of 1865 literally did not promise good prospects for a long time.

On July 12, 1865, better weather set in, but Whymper still didn't have a mountain guide to climb the mountain more safely. He suspected that an ascent was already underway at that time. In fact, it turned out that Jean-Antoine Carrel was on the road and was ambitiously trying from the Italian mountain side to be the first person to arrive at the top of the summit. Hoping, he symbolically would have celebrated the Italian unification of 1861.

Fascinating view. The Swiss north side along the Hörnligrat was to be the route of the rope team around Edward Whymper in July 1865.

Proof of picture:

https://www.kienzi.ch/flights/2008/2008-11-08.htm

Edward Whymper was in the Italian village of Breuil (today Cervinia) and, after Carrel's departure, planned to climb the Matterhorn from the Zermatt, i.e. the Swiss north side. No one can say what the first ascent would have looked like if Whymper had carried out his plan on his own. But at that very moment another Briton, the nobleman Lord Francis Douglas, came to Breuil. He was also an alpinist and was on an Alpine trip to gain experience in the European mountain world. Lord Douglas came from an ancient Scottish noble family, which was widely related to the British royal family.

He introduced himself to Whymper by saying that this was the most important topic of conversation of the renowned English Alpine Club. The Alpine Club was founded in 1857 and was intended for a better society. English nobles or large citizens were regulars here. Edward Whymper, who came from poor backgrounds, naturally hoped to become a member of the important club himself. The fact that he has already been talked about proved that he was not indifferent to the high personalities. His name made the rounds, and at least that made him an ideal part of the high assembly.

When Lord Douglas told the ambitious Whymper that he had a mountain guide in Zermatt, it was not long before they both went from Breuil to Zermatt in the Swiss canton of Valais. On the way there, they passed one of the numerous mountain farms. It belonged to the Swiss family Taugwalder. Peter Taugwalder was also a mountaineer and had worked with Edward Whymper several times. He and his son, Peter Taugwalder Jr. – at the time 22 years old – had also become curious about the Matterhorn, so that there was a Swiss-British connection between Whymper and Lord Douglas with the Taugwalders. For them, it was a fortunate circumstance that wealthy Britons financially supported the Matterhorn ascent. Nevertheless, it is unlikely that Taugwalder senior could be persuaded only because of the money to belong to the rope team of the first ascent. An old hand, as it was Taugwalder in mountaineering, loved climbing and exploring much more than the Mammon.

On the evening of July 12, 1865, the four brave ones descend to Zermatt to spend the night and the next morning to take the route towards the Matterhorn. Peter Taugwald's father was to lead the four-member rope team. His son was declared a mountain guide. Whymper in particular, but also Lord Douglas hoped that the Italians had not yet advanced far in their ascent. They placed their equipment at the chapel to pick them up very early the next morning. The domicile for one night was the Hotel Monte Rosa – still a luxurious quarter. It was named after the Monte Rosa-massif, the main tip of which is the aforementioned Dufour peak.

Lord Francis Douglas was just 19 years old in 1865. He had already climbed several peaks in the Alps and joined Edward Whymper's plan. The nobleman also had the necessary financial resources to make the first ascent of the Matterhorn possible in the first place.

Proof of picture:

Wells, Colin: A Brief History of British Mountaineering, Kumbria 2001.

Peter Taugwalder father was a very experienced mountain guide and mountaineer. He and his son were eager to climb the Matterhorn too.

Photo credit: https://de.wikipedia.org/wiki/Peter_Taugwalder#/media/Datei:Peter_Taugwalder.tiff

This sparse photograph shows Peter Taugwalder's son, who was 22 years old when he first climbed the Matterhorn.

Photo credit:

http://www.zermattbier.ch/files/images/Partnerschaft/_640x480_crop_center-center/Taugwalder_Sohn.jpg

The Hotel Monte Rosa on the right in the foreground is not far from the Matterhorn, which is covered on the left.

Photo credit:

https://www.monterosazermatt.ch/media/124195/hotel_001_boutique-hotel-zermatt_03.jpg

Upon their arrival at the hotel, Whymper and Lord Douglas noticed that other teams were meeting, who were also pursuing a plan to climb the Matterhorn. At that moment there was another coincidence:

The Reverend Charles Hudson, an English clergyman and mountaineer who was considered the best mountain guide in England at the time and was a competitor of Whymper, dined at the same time in the Monte Rosa-Hotel and also planned to climb the Matterhorn. After the meeting with Whymper and Lord Douglas, it was decided to take him and his other team with him. One of them was a British man, Douglas Hadow, who was also only 19 years old and a typical British sportsman. The aforementioned Michel Croz from Chamonix was also one of them and also tried to climb the Matterhorn.

Charles Hudson was one of the most famous British alpinists in the 19th century. Among other things, he was the first to climb the Dufour top.

Photo credit:

https://fracademic.com/pictures/frwiki/67/Charles_Hudson.jpg

Douglas Hadow was a friend of Hudson who, as a young man, was far from as experienced in the mountains as Charles Hudson or Edward Whymper. He was to play a decisive role in the accident on the Matterhorn.

Photo credit:

http://static.diepresse.com/images/uploads_380/f/d/d/4775901/hadow_1436799088699935.jpg

Michel Croz was a famous mountaineer from Chamonix. Originally he wanted to climb other mountains in July 1865, but joined Charles Hudson and Douglas Hadow.

Photo credit:

https://upload.wikimedia.org/wikipedia/commons/thumb/4/46/Michel_Croz.tiff/lossless-page1-1200px-Michel_Croz.tiff.png

The rope team was thus founded within a very short time. Seven people who had never climbed mountains together in this constellation were to climb the Matterhorn – the rough and respectful giant – together. The opinion of today's climbers is obvious: in order to make a first ascent, the participants must prepare themselves precisely and cannot unite arbitrarily. The idea of climbing the Matterhorn first was much more in focus than one's own security. It was the curiosity and excitement, but also the competition among themselves, that drove the rope team around Whymper up the mountain.

The ascent began on 13 July 1865. The visibility was good and the first part of the track could be completed surprisingly quickly. It was still possible to catch up with the Italian competitors. Edward Whymper later wrote in his book 'Scrambles Amongst the Alps' that some parts of the valley looked much more dangerous than they actually were. Of course, this allowed some altitude meters to be gained.

The rope team took a break almost 200 meters above the Hörnli Hut and decided to spend the night there. The site was explored and a tent was pitched to protect the British and Swiss from bad weather. The ropes were also checked again. Three ropes had been brought from England for the first ascent. A thin, narrow rope that was standard equipment at the time, a thicker but more unwieldy rope intended as a replacement, and a special, stretchy hemp rope from the Alpine Club with a red thread.

Over dinner, the seven climbers were confident and in a good mood. Whymper wanted to move on as soon as possible. It was his inner, energetic spirit that drove him again and again. However, he could not earn his laurels alone on this mountain tour.

On July 14th 1865, the men continued early. They still didn't use any of the three ropes. It is almost inconceivable that these men would be able to

The Hörnli-hut is now a refuge and an important station for the ascent to the Matterhorn.

Photo credit:

https://www.karcherdesign.nl/tl_files/referenzen/hoernli-huette/hoernlihuette_006_900x600.jpg

height (over 3,000 meters) without rope. In addition, temperature plays an immense role. At that time it was common to use the so-called onion model and to pull several layers on top of each other. Linen undershirts, thin shirts, thin and thicker sweaters and some thin long trousers were the standard clothes. Added to this were the shoes, which were often equipped with rivets for better stability, and an ice pick, which served as a stick and hoe in case it did not move forward in unwieldy places.

When the British-Swiss rope team was at just under 4200 meters, the geographical conditions changed. The terrain became sharper and steeper, because the ridge of the Matterhorn seems like a vertical plate here. Even Croz, who was an excellent climber through his experience, was frightened by this, and he found that something completely different began from now on. The men then decided to use the Alpine Club's special rope and connect all seven of them. This should ensure that everyone would pull together in the event of a member falling. On the other hand, at least from today's point of view, it is obvious that once two or more fell, this would bring everyone else to death.

Whymper and his teammates rushed to be definitely faster than the Italians. They changed their route from northeast to north, making it even steeper than before. As a result, the group of seven could no longer move so quickly. The climbers quickly realized that it would not continue as quickly as Whymper had hoped. The snow that covered some rocks continued to be problematic, and there were slippery spots and even cavities. That's why the climbers paid special attention to every step and at the same time to their followers. For the inexperienced Douglas Hadow, these were probably psychologically, but also technically, big hurdles. Experienced mountaineers would have left the company at the latest at such a point. Not so Edward Whymper or Michel Croz, who probably only saw the goal in front of their eyes and could not think of a reversal any more.

Suddenly, the track became unusually flat, so Whymper made a decision that would have a negative impact on this first ascent. For him, progress was far too slow. He wanted to be the first person to button up at least the last part of the route on his own. So Whymper unfastened the rope from Michel Croz – the front of the rope team – and continued to run uphill without any rope. Croz hastily followed him, but did not rush to him. Whymper later wrote in his work about his ascents to the mountains that it was not clear to him in the last meters whether he would actually finish ahead of the Italians on the top.

In the afternoon at about 13:40 it was time: Edward Whymper was the first person to climb the summit of the Matterhorn. His joy was immense, because he had been able to pursue his goal consistently. Also the others of the rope team arrived at the highest point at 4478 meters above NN.

It was an indescribable feeling to be the first to stand on a seemingly indomitable peak. Whymper saw the Italians, who were much further away than he had assumed. He shouted to the Italians that it was too late for them and rejoiced in his victory. What a relief for Whymper! Since Carrel did not seem to understand what was being called to him, Whymper threw a few stones down the slope to indicate that he was the first climber. The Italians descended on Breuil disappointed to tell their compatriots that they had not made it. Out of ambition, Carrel decided to reach the top of the Matterhorn a few days after the first ascent, which he and his team succeeded in doing.

The British-Swiss rope team remained on the summit for an hour and gradually changed its name. Peter Taugwalder father was particularly proud that he had made it to the mountain with his son. But he was concerned about how they could go back safely and stable together. After all, there were people in the rope team like Douglas Hadow, who had not yet had much experience in mountaineering.

It was about 3pm in the afternoon when Croz, Hadow, Hudson and Lord Douglas made their way back. Instead of waiting for the others, they joined a rope in four. Edward Whymper made some sketches so that he could later show them to his publisher. He also wrote the names of the first climbers on a piece of paper and locked them in a bottle.

The view from the Matterhorn is majestic. The feeling and the idea of being the first people on this summit and climbing it with such a loosely bound rope team was certainly indescribable for all involved.

Photo credit: https://upload.wikimedia.org/wikipedia/commons/b/be/Dent_d%27Hérens_from_the_Matterhorn.jpg

Meanwhile, Taugwalder father made his way back and joined the four previous alpinists. In the end, Whymper and Taugwalder son followed, who lined up in pairs and thus walked part of the route.

No one was waiting for the other, so the competitive idea was probably predominant again. Why else should the climbers go downhill separately? Taugwald's father soon caught up so quickly that he connected with Lord Douglas with the thin auxiliary rope. Whymper and Taugwalder Sohn also made good progress and teamed up with Taugwalder Father together. The rope team was complete again from now on, but they climbed downhill without real stopping at the rocks. The proposal to place the ropes around some of the rocky outcrops to ensure a more stable hold was not heard. So the men slowly went downhill one step at a time. For Douglas Hadow, this was certainly a terrible feeling.

The drawing by Edward Whymper shows Whymper and Croz when they arrived on the mountain. What is astonishing is how detailed Whymper was drawing the rocks and the people. He was truly a good illustrator.

Photo credit:

http://cdn2.spiegel.de/images/image-866795-galleryV9-ajod.jpg

The idea that all seven were hanging on a rope, thus significantly restricting the freedom of movement, so that the human body was in a rigid state, is terrible. The young Hadow in particular was in a state of fear, so Croz helped him to set his foot safely. But Hadow slipped on a smooth surface and fell into the abyss. Michel Croz, Charles Hudson and Lord Douglas also fell. Michel Croz, Whymper wrote later, was still hanging from a rock slab and screaming that he couldn't hold on. Then he, too, plunged into the depths.

Whymper and the two Taugwalders were paralyzed when they heard the screams of their comrades. They shouted the names of their fallen comrades, but received no response. It took them quite a while to realize that it was too late and that the mountain had lived up to its name as a rough rock. Whymper wrote in his book about the Alps that the Taugwalders cried and were desperate. The Briton seemed to be in the spotlight again, because it would be inconceivable if even a rough man like Whymper showed no emotion in such a situation

When they gathered again after a long time, the two Taugwalders and Whymper set out on the further way back. They stayed on a rock slab and didn't say another word to each other. At this point Whymper wrote that he too had trembled all over the body and became aware that it could also hit him. Seven times he had already climbed the Matterhorn, he had repeatedly failed and fell 60 meters into the depths. This time, especially after the devastating accident, he wanted to get back to the valley safely.

Around noon on July 15, 1865, the three alpinists reached Zermatt. People quickly understood that something was wrong, and immediately the question of guilt came to the fore, which still touches the story of the first ascent today. With the first ascent of the Matterhorn, the end of the Golden Age of Alpinism was sealed (for the time being).

The bodies were searched over the next two days. The identities could be identified using bags and jacket scraps. However, the body of Lord Francis Douglas has never been found. Even Queen Victoria intervened by forbade future alpine tours, as the British blood was too valuable for it to be shed in the mountains.

On 21 July 1865, a court hearing took place in a Zermatt hotel. However, this was managed by a hotelier, so that the negotiation was carried out by laymen. First, Edward Whymper was asked about the story of the departure from the Tent camp above the Hörnli Hut began. He said Hadow had had big problems on the way back and Croz helped him. However, Hadow slipped and dragged Croz and the other two into the abyss. Because Taugwalder son and Whymper pulled so the rope, Taugwalder father could be kept so that he did not fall along. This force, which lay on the rope, had resulted in the rope between Taugwalder father and Lord Douglas cracking.

Queen Victoria, who reigned from 1837 to 1901, came from the German House of the Welfs. When the disaster on the Matterhorn occurred in 1865 and a distant family member died, she forbade the English to undertake such expeditions in the future.

Photo credit:

https://i.pinimg.com/originals/18/a8/77/18a8772fd914e8c928ae28b9a718c64e.jpg

The Frenchman Gustave Duré (1832-1883) made a lithograph on which he painted the misfortune on the Matterhorn.

Photo credit:

https://www.aargauerzeitung.ch/schweiz/150-jahre-erstbesteigung-die-tragoedie-nach-dem-gipfelsturm-129325411#fullscreen=true&galleryAssetId=129325433&imageAssetId=129325431

After the trial with Whymper, Peter Taugwalder father was summoned to describe his version. He was burdened with major problems, as he himself was a mountain guide and thus had to bear a greater responsibility. He testified that the evening before the ascent in Zermatt he had warned the other mountaineers that two mountain guides (Croz and he) were too few. Since Whymper and Hudson had said that they too would be well versed in steep terrain, the discussion about it ended.

Taugwalder father also reported that Michel Croz had taken over the approach. The way back was made with the special rope of the Alpine Club and not with the thicker, more unwieldy rope. Taugwalder father approached Lord Douglas and waited for Whymper and Taugwalder son, who were also connected to the thin rope. According to Peter Taugwalder, this rope was still stable enough to hold it together. At the moment of the crash, he had wrapped the thin rope between Whymper and him around a rocky outcrop. Why did he use a thin rope to connect? Taugwalder father justifies himself by the fact that the special rope of the Alpine Club was too short to hang on to it. It has to be said that the thin ropes were standard ropes at the time. The British, through their seafaring history, knew more about the tear resistance of various ropes since the 16th century, which is why they brought these ropes into the mountains.

Peter Taugwalder testified to the court that he firmly believed that if the rope had not been torn, he could have held the others together with Croz. Anyone who has ever been to the mountains and fallen on a medium-divided ski slope know show tedious it is to get straight stop again. Now such an accident happens on the Matterhorn, and also in a steep place – how could the climbers have kept each other? The mountain is of course the stronger, which is especially evident in such places.

The statement about the stop of the followers was also strange because Croz also fell. How could Croz have supported the other three above him? Did Taugwalder think he could have held Lord Douglas and Croz Douglas Hadow? Even this is not possible in such places with such an unfavourable fuse.

In the village, Taugwalder father was admired by many people, but there were also some who loathed him or even envied him. Even the pastor from the Zermatt church repeatedly emphasized to Taugwalder that he was against such mountain climbs from the beginning. Taugwalders shouldrather stay with their cows on the mountain farm thanclimb pointlessly.

In a further court hearing there were interviews about the differences in the statements of Whymper and Taugwalder. Taugwalder still stood by his statement that he was able to save his son, Whymper, and himself through the rope, which he tied around a rock at the decisive moment. His intransigent attitude led to a rope rift between Taugwalder and Lord Douglas. Whymper, who, like Taugwalder, believed that Douglas Hadow was in fact only an amateur in the mountain world, held the same opinion.

The Zermatt court ruled that the incident was a tragic accident caused by Douglas Hadow. That is a very vague insinuation. The responsibility for inviting Douglas Hadow as Hudson's friend on this tour was not solely his responsibility. It could also have been that Charles

The torn rope, which is now on display at the Matterhorn Museum in Zermatt, still raises questions today.

Photo credit:

https://www.welt.de/img/vermischtes/mobile168079845/1872504287-ci102l-w1024/150-Jahre-Erstbesteigung-des-Matterhorns.jpg

The shoe of Lord Douglas, whose body was never found, point to better stability through the special nails.

Photo credit:

https://storytelling.nzz.ch/2015/matterhorn/data/images/320/21.jpg

The shoe of Douglas Hadow looks more like a shoe, that is made for a walk. From today's point of view, it is therefore even more daring and dangerous to climb such a steep mountain with such shoes without nails.

Photo credit:

https://storytelling.nzz.ch/2015/matterhorn/data/images/1600/24.jpg

Hudson, for example, had not kept the rope tight enough and that the accident had happened. Was it really the rope that was torn? Or was it possibly cut? Of course, questions immediately arose for the press. That wasn't much different then than it is today. The press was hungry for stories. Once a message has found some continuity, it is no longer usable. But as soon as rumours, conjectures and other talk come to light, they are immediately disseminated in all media.

The Wiener Neue Freie Presse published a large article about the auxiliary rope and the experienced Edward Whymper. It claimed that he may have cut the rope between Lord Douglas and Taugwalder during the fall. In such a situation, however, to think about it at all and to walk down within seconds in order to quickly cut the rope at the front man would not only be irresponsible, but also seems unlikely.

In Interlaken, where Whymper went immediately after the trial, people barely recognized him. He is said to have been very pale and pale and looked very distraught. According to this article, murder could well have been the new accusation. This was followed by the death penalty in the canton of Valais, which is why Whymper was all the more unhappy about these events.

The material researcher Paul Smith from Zurich examined the rope from the muse in connection with a documentation of the SRF about the first ascent of the Matterhorn. In fact, the fiber ends seem far too straight to be a crack. Should Whymper, who was much higherup in Taugwalder's statement about the incident, have cut the rope? That would be very difficult on such a steep terrain. In the short time, from today's point of view, it is much closer that Taugwalder's father cut the rope. He was in an extremely delicate position, which is why he slid the rope around a rock to ensure better support for himself and the backers. In this situation, he could have realized that four people were already falling and that he and the other two climbers could also be pulled to their deaths at any time. So he grabbed the knife and cut the rope.

The mysterious questions cannot be fully answered. Whymper took the torn rope to the UK after the fall. It is not clear how it ended up in the Zermatt Museum.

For the said documentary 'Death on the Matterhorn – The tragic story of the first ascent' a original rope was woven. It was subjected to a test to show how much mass the rope is tearing. The result is clear: the rope tears at about 300 kilograms of load. From today's point of view, it is therefore closest to the fact that the conscious, very thin rope between Taugwalder and Lord Douglas also cracked.

Edward Whymper withdrew from the public eye for the time being and wrote his already mentioned book, in which he blames Peter Taugwalder, among others, for the accident. It was he who had deliberately chosen the thinner rope. Whymper accused Taugwalder of deliberate negligence because he wanted to protect himself in case the first four alpinists were to fall. Taugwalder set it up in such a way that the climbers in front of him used the weak rope. To insinuate such a thing to a poor Swiss mountain farmer is, in fact, almost iniquitous. Through these statements Whymper also ensured that the hitherto good reputation of Peter Taugwalder father was damaged. This is problematic because none of the Taugwalders had published their views in any document. Presumably they could hardly read and write.

Peter Taugwalder father became increasingly depressed. His wife had already died a few years earlier, and in 1867 his second son Josef died, who was originally also supposed to be present at the first ascent, but had returned to the village after consultation with the other alpinists. Taugwald's father was plagued by severe, certainly unnecessary feelings of guilt. Whymper's statement that he was mentally confused and no longer capable as a mountain guide did not let him go for the rest of his life. As a consequence, few, soon no more guests came to him to climb with Taugwaldmountains.

Whymper went on to write that the Taugwalders had complained during the descent that they would not receive any money for this expedition, at least for the time being, because their financiers had crashed. Edward Whymper had offered to pay the two Taugwalders, but they refused and told Whymper that he would rather tell the newspapers that they would no longer be paid. This, too, is rather unlikely, because the Taugwalders had in mind first and foremost mountaineering and not capital. Sure, money played a role, and it is likely that both were concerned about how things should go on financially, but it is unlikely that they would have behaved so strangely towards Whymper. However, it is questionable why Peter Taugwalder did not tie the rope of the Alpine Club to himself. Was it really too short?

The British pioneer Sir Arnold Lunn suggested in the last century that Edward Whymper had cut the rope. However, this did not happen on departure, but shortly before he reached the summit. Whymper told a British author at a dinner that he had cut the rope to be more mobile and to be able to walk the route alone and faster.

Edward Whymper conceals the rope cut in his story of the ascent. Instead, he accuses Peter Taugwalder father of having evil intentions or of knowing the danger of the thin rope. But he couldn't do anything about it, because he took the thin rope only because there was no other one at the time of departure. The thicker rope was worn by Michel Croz, the first in the series. The rope of the Alpine Club was probably too short and divided into two parts.

Display of the ropes at the end:

1-2-3-4---5-6-7

The simple strokes between points 1, 2, 3 and 4 and between points 5, 6 and 7 represent the same rope pieces, since Whymper splits the rope. It was the more powerful rope of the Alpine Club. Michel Croz (1), Douglas Hadow (2), Charles Hudson (3) and Lord Douglas (4) were associated with this, as well as Peter Taugwalder's father (5), Edward Whymper (6) and Peter Taugwalder (7).

The connection between Lord Douglas and Peter Taugwalder was the thin rope (marked here with three lines). The thicker, more unwieldy rope probably carried Michel Croz with him.

Whymper's book was a clear success, but not for the Taugwalders. Just because Whymper had the means to market his story of the Matterhorn, of course, this was no reason to write so negatively about his mountain comrades. Especially as a survivor, more respect would have been needed at such a point.

Peter Taugwalder father then emigrated to North America for a few years in order to gain distance. However, he returned to Switzerland and helped with the construction of the Hotel Schwarzsee. Peter Taugwalder died in July 1888 at the age of 68.

Edward Whymper was a wealthy man after the success of his books; nevertheless, he did not become a member of the higher society. He married, divorced again and remained essentially a loner. Whymper died in his hotel room in Chamonix on September 16, 1911, at the age of 71. Edward Whymper probably wasn't happy after the story on the Matterhorn. His funeral was a great ceremony. People from France and Switzerland paid his last respects.

The name Whymper is still advertised in Zermatt today. After the tragedy on the Matterhorn, despite the Queen's ban, many British tourists and alpinists came to Zermatt, making the city a brand name. The Taugwalders, on the other hand, went unnoticed for a long time. The descendants of the Taugwalder family also brought a plaque in Zermatt with the memory of two family members who climbed the great mountain of Switzerland for the first time. Taugwalder Sohn remained active as a mountain guide throughout his life and accompanied many of those arriving on their way to the Matterhorn. Taugwald's father is said to have once told him that it was a pity that Whymper survived and not the likeable Lord Douglas. "Matterhorn Peter", as Taugwald's son was later called, climbed the Matterhorn more than a hundred times before he died in 1923 at the age of 80.

Despite the circumstances, all seven climbers are still in the memory today. In order to keep it that way, this small commemorative letter is intended to commemorate the seven alpinists who managed to climb such a mountain. This should be the main focus and not the disputes between Whymper and the Taugwalders. May the courage of the Seven be remembered for a long time and not be disputed about rumours.

The plaque in Zermatt is reminiscent of the two Taugwalders who also climbed the Matterhorn as the first people ever to climb.

Photo credit:

http://dbsevice.toubiz.de/var/plain_site/storage/images/orte/zermatt/haus-taugwalder/poi/1625787-1-ger-DE/Poi_front_large.jpg

He will probably remain in the memory of the Swiss and English for a long time: Edward Whymper, whose plaque hangs on the Hotel Monte Rosa.

Photo credit:

https://spimages.summitpost.org/228444.jpg?auto=format&fit=max&h=800&ixlib=php-2.1.1&q=35&s=8020fe7689aac418bafa167c0fba5dc2

References

Apart from Whymper's work, there is not much scientific literature about the first ascent of the Matterhorn. The booklet was created using Whymper's publication and the Swiss documentation of the SRF of 2015 mentioned here, which he filmed on the occasion of the 150th anniversary. The story can be found on all websites, especially on Swiss sites.

See also:

Grupp, Peter: Faszination Berg. Die Geschichte des Alpinismus, Cologne and Others 2008.

Whymper, Edward: Scrambles Amongst the Alps, London 1871.

General links:

https://www.diepresse.com/4775901/matterhorn-1865-und-das-goldene-zeitalter-des-alpinismus, last called: Nov 27, 2019.

https://www.matterhornparadise.ch/de/Entdecken/Region/Matterhorn, last called: Nov 27, 2019.

https://www.spiegel.de/geschichte/matterhorn-erstbesteigung-1865-wettrennen-endet-in-tragoedie-a-1042799.html, last called: Nov 27, 2019.

https://www.welt.de/geschichte/article143832008/Die-dramatische-Erstbesteigung-des-Matterhorns.html, last called: Nov 27, 2019.

https://www.zermattportal.de/matterhorn/erstbesteigung+matterhorn/last accessed: Nov 27, 2019

Link of the documentation:

https://www.youtube.com/watch?v=1POp3fsIsF8, last called: Nov 27, 2019.

Memory

First and foremost, it commemorates the dead who lost their lives on the Matterhorn on 14 July 1865. Their alpinist achievements should never be forgotten.

Michel Croz (1830–1865), Douglas Hadow (1846–1865)

Charles Hudson (1828–1865)

Lord Francis Douglas (1847–1865)

The memory also goes to the British alpinist Edward Whymper (1840-1911), who is very controversial with his statements about the Taugwalder, but is unforgotten by his activities and his successes in the mountains.

Finally, Peter Taugwalder father (1820-1888) and Peter Taugwalder Sohn (1843-1923) are mentioned. After the tragedy on the Matterhorn, Taugwalder father fell into unjust disrepute. His son led even more curious people to the Matterhorn until his death. They, too, remain unforgotten.

Acknowledgement

A big thank you goes to my family, who give me the opportunity to talk about all the historical events. I would especially like to thank my dear mother, who not only has an open ear for historical events all the time, but was able to inspire me for the mountain world in all winter holidays as a young boy.

I would also like to thank my friend Florian Albert, with whom I have discussed the myth Matterhorn many times. It was not self-evident that he took these conversations.